The Thinking Girl's Treasury of Real Princesses

Sorghaghtani of Mongolia

Series editor **Shirin Yim Bridges**
Consulting editor **Amy Novesky**
Copy editor **Jennifer Fry**
Book design **Jay Mladjenovic**

Typeset mainly in Samarkan and Volkswagen TS
Illustrations rendered in pen and watercolor

Manufactured in Singapore

Library of Congress PCN 2010903615

First Edition   10 9 8 7 6 5 4 3 2 1

Goosebottom Books LLC
710 Portofino Lane, Foster City CA 94404

www.goosebottombooks.com

For Tiegan and Alena, the original Thinking Girl
and the real Fairy-Monkey Princess.

~ Shirin Yim Bridges ~

For my family and friends.

~ Albert Nguyen ~

The Thinking Girl's Treasury of Real Princesses

Hatshepsut of Egypt

Artemisia of Caria

Sorghaghtani of Mongolia

Qutlugh Terkan Khatun of Kirman

Isabella of Castile

Nur Jahan of India

sorghaghtani of mongolia

By Shirin Yim Bridges | Illustrated by Albert Nguyen

goosebottombooks

She was called what?!

The names in this book can be hard to pronounce, and if you've ever heard Mongolian spoken, you'll know that no English pronunciation guide is going to be of any help!

Here are most of the unusual names in this book, broken down so that you can say them. (Just don't expect to be understood by a Mongolian person.) You can also hear some of these names pronounced on the website www.merriam-webster.com/dictionary.

Try it, it's neat.

Genghis	geng•giss
Sorghaghtani	sork•gak•tah•nee
Kereit	ker•rate
Tolui	tol•loo•ee
Mongke	mong•keh
Hulegu	hoo•lay•goo
Kublai	koo•bleh
Arik-Boke	ah•rick•boh•keh
Koumiss	koo•miss
Ogodei	oh•geh•day
Guyuk	guy•yook
Ebuskan	eb•boos•khan
Chagatai	chug•gah•tie
Kuriltai	queue•rill•tie

sorghaghtani of mongolia

When Genghis Khan and his Mongols swept out of the east around 800 years ago, conquering all before them and putting whole cities to the sword, the western world thought that they were the devil's horsemen. The Mongols were said to eat dead bodies, leaving only bones, and to make their favorite lunch out of old or ugly women.

The truth was a little different. The Mongols did not eat women for lunch (or breakfast, or dinner). They respected their women, and often trusted them to rule the new lands they'd conquered. In particular, the Mongols admired one princess. She had proven herself a wise and able ruler, taking lands that had been ruined by war and making them wealthy again, and bringing mutual respect and cooperation to a downtrodden and distrustful people. She was ambitious; she did not exactly steal the imperial throne, but in a battle of wits that was like a giant chess game, she won it! And, she carefully taught and raised four sons who would conquer half the world. Her name was Sorghaghtani, and this is her story.

Where she lived

Genghis Khan, conquerer of half the world, rose out of nothing. His father, the leader of a minor Mongol tribe, had been murdered when Genghis was just a young boy. Unprotected, Genghis was captured and enslaved, managing to escape only because a guard took pity on him. From these unlikely beginnings, and in a remarkably short period of time, Genghis united all the Mongol tribes beneath him and began the conquest of the largest contiguous empire the world has ever seen. (Contiguous means within a single boundary. The British Empire was larger in land mass, but it was made up of unconnected bits and pieces scattered all over the globe.)

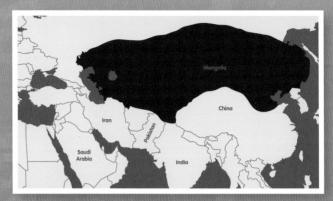

Genghis' empire at the time of his death.

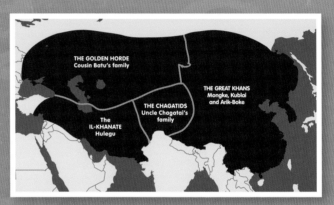

The expanded empire of Sorghaghtani's sons and their cousins.

When she lived

This timeline shows when the other princesses in The Thinking Girl's Treasury of Real Princesses once lived.

1500BC	500BC	1200AD	1300AD	1400AD	1600AD
Hatshepsut of Egypt	Artemisia of Caria	Sorghaghtani of Mongolia	Qutlugh Terkan Khatun	Isabella of Castile	Nur Jahan of India

her story

Sorghaghtani was a princess of the Kereit tribe, one of many tribes that inhabited the sweeping grasslands north of China. When she was very young, maybe eleven or twelve, she was married to Tolui, a son of Genghis Khan. Tolui was himself only 10 years old at the time. (The Mongols married young, but this was young even by their standards! Girls were usually married around 16, and were often a little older than their husbands.)

Six years later, when Sorghaghtani was still a teenager, she gave birth to the couple's first son, Mongke. Three more sons, Hulegu, Kublai, and Arik-Boke soon followed.

Sorghaghtani's husband, Prince Tolui, was by Mongolian tradition the "Prince of the Hearth." He was the youngest son in his family, and earmarked to inherit the ancestral lands. But this did not keep Tolui close to home. He was often away fighting as one of his father's generals, and was, in fact, the prince who conquered more lands than any other.

What was Sorghaghtani's life like, left behind with her young children? The Golden Family (all those of, or married to, Genghis' blood) did not live in palaces, but followed the traditional nomadic way of life, living in tents or *gers*.

Sorghaghtani and her young sons would have lived in a round ger, maybe 30 feet wide, made of felt stretched on a wicker frame. The door was always positioned to face south. On the opposite side of the ger — the north — was Tolui's often-empty bed. To the east was the women's area, where Sorghaghtani and her maidens worked and chatted through the day. The west was where male visitors were made comfortable and welcome. This side of the ger was also where the four little boys hung up their bows and quivers and laid down their bedding for the night.

Sorghaghtani's ger would have been surrounded by the gers of royal relatives, attendants, officials, and guards — because this moveable village was, after all, the Mongol court. As a flower attracts bees, the court drew to it the dignitaries and ambassadors of many foreign countries, most of whom now had to bow to the Mongols as masters. They came to conduct their business with Genghis and his princes, or if the men were away, with their wives. From here, decisions were made that affected the lives of people as far away as Japan, Java, and Austria, and Sorghaghtani had a role in making them. For example, she reorganized the way taxes were collected in Tolui's lands, increasing the amount that made it into the Golden Family's hands.

Just like any nomadic group, when it came time to find better pasture for their animals, the whole court packed up and moved. Sorghaghtani's household alone needed more than 100 carts to move all their gers and possessions — the gers perched fully assembled on top of the carts, the Mongolian version of mobile homes. Every few months, these long and odd-looking caravans lumbered slowly across the plains, raising clouds of dust and surrounded by great herds of horses, sheep, and oxen.

It was the women who decided when to move, and where to move to. Women repaired the carts and loaded the camels. Women harnessed the carts to oxen teams, hitched them one behind the other, then drove the entire train from the cart in front. Women rode as sentries, laughing and high-spirited, bows slung over their shoulders and quivers bristling with arrows. Mongolian women were independent and capable, and Sorghaghtani laughed and rode among them.

The Golden Family

Genghis' family — the Golden Family — literally ruled half the world. This family tree shows only family members who have appeared in our story. (The khans often had more than one wife and many children, so the entire Golden Family would not all fit on one page!)

Horizontal lines mean "married to." Vertical lines mean "descended from." The names of the Great Khans appear in bold.

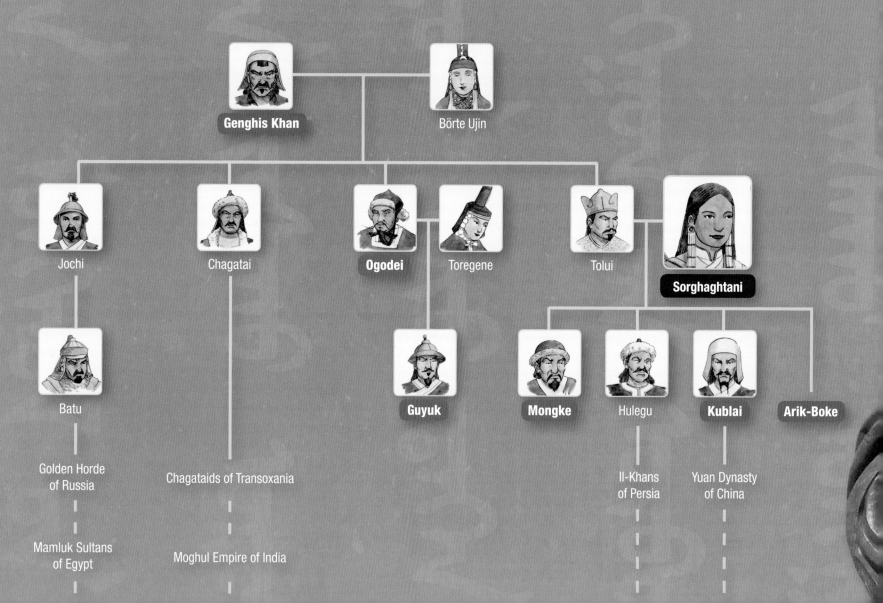

By 1227, Genghis Khan had forged an empire that stretched from the Caspian Sea in the west, to the Sea of Japan in the east. To do this, his armies had fought more enemy nations than any other army had before or since. That year, Genghis suffered a bad fall from his horse. Wracked with fever from his internal injuries, he commanded his sons and grandsons to remain loyal to each other and to continue their world conquest. Then, the legendary Genghis Khan died.

Only four years later, Sorghaghtani suffered an even more personal loss. One morning, after drinking the alcoholic fermented mare's milk called *koumiss* all night, Tolui dropped dead at the age of 40. It must have been a shock to lose the man who'd been her partner since the age of 10. Even if he had often been away, and even though he'd often been drunk when he was home (all of Genghis' sons were big drinkers), Sorghaghtani and Tolui had grown up together, had children together, governed a territory together. But in addition to the personal blow, Tolui's death now exposed Sorghaghtani and her sons to danger.

At first, all seemed well enough. On Tolui's death his brother, the Great Khan Ogodei, made Sorghaghtani the official ruler of all of Tolui's lands. This was a mark of personal respect for Sorghaghtani, especially as her eldest son, Mongke, was already old enough to rule. But then, Ogodei tried to marry Sorghaghtani to his son, Guyuk. He hoped in this way to absorb Sorghaghtani's domains. Sorghaghtani firmly turned down the offer. She explained that she was too busy educating her four sons to have time for another man.

▲ A Persian miniature painting showing Sorghaghtani and Prince Tolui together.

What she wore

The greatest change to Mongolian dress (before the recent move to sweaters, jackets, T-shirts, and jeans) actually occurred during Sorghaghtani's lifetime. Their new empire made the Mongols wealthy. Dull, homespun woollens were replaced by imported silks, satins, embroideries, and brocades, in rich and bright colors.

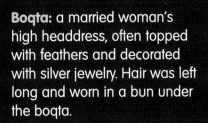

Boqta: a married woman's high headdress, often topped with feathers and decorated with silver jewelry. Hair was left long and worn in a bun under the boqta.

Long tassel earrings.

Short sleeved jackets or waistcoats were worn over the deel, often in contrasting colors.

Gutul: elaborately decorated leather boots. The upturned toes were supposed to keep feet warmer in winter by allowing a little air pocket for insulation. In winter, gutul were worn with felt socks and fur covers called degtii.

Deel: a long robe with a slanting collar fastened under the right shoulder, and long sleeves that acted as gloves. Sorghaghtani's would have been made from imported silk and bordered by rich brocades.

Married women did not wear the *bus*, a cloth sash or belt tied over the deel to emphasize the waist.

Underneath the deel, often tucked into the boots, women wore trousers.

It was true that Sorghaghtani took the raising of her sons very seriously. She took the time to teach them herself and by example. In addition to ruling nearly all of Mongolia, Sorghaghtani was now the ruler of part of northern China. This land had been ruined and mostly deserted during Genghis' wars of conquest, and the people who remained were rightly terrified and distrustful of their new Mongol overlords.

Sorghaghtani set about restoring the area to its former wealth. Instead of bringing in Mongol officials who thought all of China should be turned into pasture for horses, she appointed local officials, watching them closely but treating them with respect. She worked with them to improve harvests, investing in community projects like irrigation and drainage. She made taxes and their collection fair. Bit by bit, she won the trust of the people, who began to return to the area to start farming again — and when they did, they paid taxes, which built Sorghaghtani's wealth.

This lesson on the value of cooperation, mutual respect, and tolerance of other cultures, was absorbed by all of her sons, who would grow up to be known for their ability to recognize and reward talent regardless of race or religion. (Kublai, in fact, borrowed not only her ideas but some of her Chinese officials to reorganize his own lands.) Sorghaghtani drew praise not only for her wisdom and good government, but because she'd raised sons who were more than strong individuals — they were a unified team.

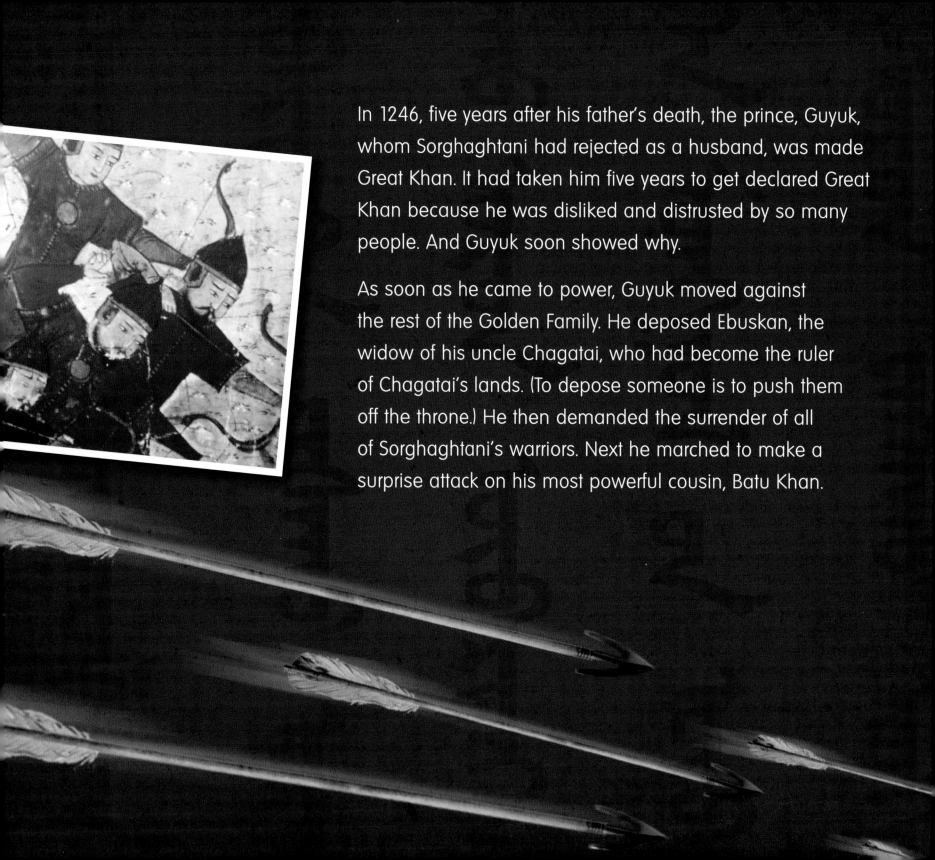

In 1246, five years after his father's death, the prince, Guyuk, whom Sorghaghtani had rejected as a husband, was made Great Khan. It had taken him five years to get declared Great Khan because he was disliked and distrusted by so many people. And Guyuk soon showed why.

As soon as he came to power, Guyuk moved against the rest of the Golden Family. He deposed Ebuskan, the widow of his uncle Chagatai, who had become the ruler of Chagatai's lands. (To depose someone is to push them off the throne.) He then demanded the surrender of all of Sorghaghtani's warriors. Next he marched to make a surprise attack on his most powerful cousin, Batu Khan.

Sorghaghtani acted quickly. In what became something like a giant chess game played at high speed, she sent a message to Batu to warn him of the attack, possibly saving Batu's life. They made a deal. This deal might have included the murder of Guyuk, who died rather mysteriously on his way to depose his cousin. Before Guyuk's family could respond, Batu then called a kuriltai, the traditional coming together of all the Mongol tribes to name a new Great Khan. At this, fulfilling Batu's part of the deal, Sorghaghtani's eldest son, Mongke, was proclaimed supreme ruler of the Mongols, instead of the older and more powerful Batu.

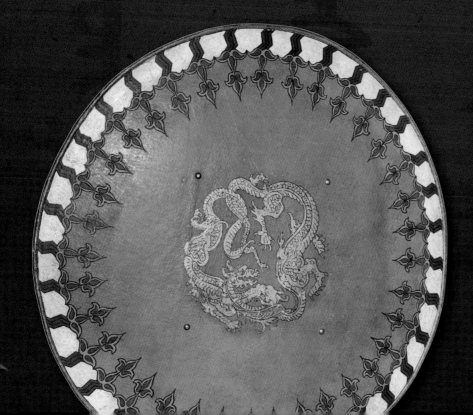

▲ Every Mongol warrior had a Spirit Banner, made by tying the hairs of his best stallions to the shaft of a spear. The banner marked the identity of the warrior while he was alive, and was thought to hold his spirit after his death. Genghis Khan had two spirit banners — a white one for use in times of peace, and a black one for times of war.

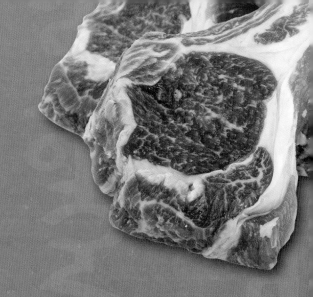

But, Guyuk's family had boycotted the kuriltai, protesting that it wasn't valid because it had met outside Mongolia. Sorghaghtani acted swiftly again. She called a kuriltai in the ancestral lands that she controlled, where Genghis Khan himself had been elected. Nobody could refuse to attend and respect a kuriltai that met there! The Mongol tribes reassembled. Once more they proclaimed Mongke as the Great Khan. Guyuk's sons, who had planned to launch a surprise attack during the celebrations, were arrested and executed. By the end of Sorghaghtani's chess game, her family was firmly in power.

Sorghaghtani must have been very proud to see her eldest son confirmed as the Great Khan with his three brothers standing by him as generals. She must have looked forward to guiding them all as their most trusted advisor. But sadly, Sorghaghtani's influence — and her enjoyment of her sons' successes — was cut short by her death, from unknown causes, only one year later.

What she ate

The Mongols were famous for being able to endure hardship, and that included a tough diet. Mongol horsemen were said to feed themselves with raw meat kept under their saddles. The rubbing of the saddle made the meat tender enough to eat raw, and the meat in turn protected the horses from saddle sores. But there is no doubt that the Mongols also liked a good feast. When Mongke was made Great Khan, he and Sorghaghtani threw a week-long party. They fed their guests 300 horses and oxen, 3,000 sheep, and 2,000 wagons of koumiss!

an impressive legacy

Having learned from his mother the value of cooperation, Mongke Great Khan went on to share his empire with his brothers and his cousins. He restored the lands that Guyuk had stolen to his uncle Chagatai's family, and left his mother's ally, his cousin Batu, to rule his domain in peace.

Hulegu, the most fearsome warrior of these formidable brothers, extended the Mongol empire to the southwest. He founded a new dynasty — the Il-Khans of Persia (and became a relative by marriage to one of the princesses in this treasury, Qutlugh Terkan Khatun). Like his mother, he was expert at appointing local governors to work with him.

Sorghaghtani's third son, Kublai, completed the conquest of China, annexed parts of Southeast Asia, and launched several invasions of Japan. He showed his mother's respect for different cultures by embracing that of China, and founding his own dynasty there, the Yuan. Kublai became Great Khan after Mongke died.

The youngest brother, Arik-Boke, was a Prince of the Hearth who stayed closer to home. But he claimed, at least for a while, the title of Great Khan, so he wasn't entirely left out of the glory.

Mongke, Hulegu, Kublai, and Arik-Boke got their chance to rewrite world history because of the shrewdness of their mother. They were never in direct line for the throne, and the fact that they inherited it at all was due to this wily and capable princess.